Not From Here

A Spiritual Misfit's Guide

TO FINDING PURPOSE AND BELONGING

Laura Rain

PUBLISHED BY FIDELI PUBLISHING, INC.

Copyright © 2024 by Laura Rain

All rights reserved.

No part of this book may be reproduced in any form or by any electronic or mechanical means including information storage and retrieval systems without permission in writing from the publisher, except by a reviewer, who may quote brief passages in a review.

Fideli Publishing, Inc.
119 W Morgan St.
Martinsville, IN 46151
888-343-3542
www.FideliPublishing.com

Cover design by artist Victoria Williams Steen

Photo credits: back cover, Mike J. Arledge; author photo, Andee Marley

ISBN: 978-1-60414-997-5 (soft cover)

Visit the author's website @
www.holisticspiritualcounseling.com

PRINTED IN THE UNITED STATES OF AMERICA

Dear Reader,

I first received the inspiration to write a book on the topic of spiritual misfits in the fall of 2012 after hearing many people describe their experiences and feelings to me of "*not being from here*" and a longing to "*go home, wherever that is*". Although I did not identify with being a writer, I chose to listen to the call; a nudge from Spirit, to write this book. I began writing at a writer's retreat in South Carolina in March of 2013. The Atlantic ocean, in particular, has always been a place of deep spiritual connection for me; a place of belonging as I feel in no other place. As synchronicity would have it, the room I had been originally assigned at the retreat center ended up being inhabitable due to an unforeseen issue; and I was lucky enough to be put up at a hotel with a seaside room, right on the beach. As I opened my laptop to begin writing, I allowed the rhythm of the ocean waves to move through me; to carry me as I began to write this book.

Fast forward a year and a half to December of 2014. It was two months after my 40th birthday when I became unexpectedly, miraculously pregnant. I had been told years before by a fertility specialist that I could never have a child. I had always felt one of my purposes in this life would be to be a mom, so this news was devastating. I was an involved stepmom and had created a beautiful family life with my husband, Michael. Grieving and surrendering my desire to be a biological mom and accepting my life just the way it was became my new spiritual practice. Just when I felt like I had reached a place within myself of letting go and having truly surrendered, this miracle pregnancy occurred. My husband and I were thrilled beyond measure. I continued to write the book with the goal in mind that it would be published in 2017. In September of 2015, my beautiful son was born. I continued to write as I balanced becoming a new mom with all the other demands of life, family, and work. My new goal of publishing the book became 2020.

In December 2019, I finished the book and it was ready for publication! (As finished as it could be, anyway. I think I'm not alone in the sense that just about every writer out there would agree that they never feel

Dear Reader

---

quite finished with their books; that there is always something that they could make better, but at some point, one has to decide that the book is good enough and that it's so much better to be out in the world imperfect than it is to sit on one's laptop!) What a great metaphor for life, right? We have to be willing to put ourselves out there, as we are, as imperfect beings, in order to make a difference in this world!

In the beginning of 2020, I excitedly worked toward all the things that one has to do to launch a book, including scheduling a book launch. I decided on a launch date: March 20, 2020. It felt so right. All the details were falling into place. It was an exciting time. For me, as an introvert who suffers from a slight amount of social anxiety, I put on my extrovert hat and was out in the world being a mover and shaker, a marketing machine, a networking goddess; a new budding author on the brink of her debut!

It was the week of March 20, 2020. The Covid-19 pandemic was upon us. My home city of Indianapolis issued a stay at home order. The book launch was canceled. I closed my spiritual counseling office and shifted to an all virtual practice. My kids came home from school and didn't go back until August of 2021. The boxes of books I had purchased for the launch were put on a shelf. After many attempts of rescheduling the event during the early days of the pandemic, to have it still not be the right time, I gave up. I was disappointed and disheartened. We moved homes. I lost the balance in myself and my life. I found myself immersed in the virtual homeschooling world with my special needs stepdaughter and my young son. It was challenging, overwhelming, and stressful. I had very little time or space for self-care. I found myself suffering from severe caregiver burnout, grieving my old life, and having a difficult time adjusting in my new life.

In August 2021, my kids went back to in-person school. Hooray! I opened up a new office to be able to see clients in person again. Life began to take on a resemblance of a balanced life. I spent the fall of 2021 feeling super grateful, taking care of myself more, and doing the things I needed to do to restore myself from my caregiver burnout. For me, this looked like spending time with friends, allowing myself to sleep more, rest more, exercise more, receive massage, acupuncture, chiropractic care, and therapy. I began to feel more rested, resourced, and replenished. I started to feel like myself again.

At the time of this writing, it is the beginning of 2022. So much has changed in our world and in myself

Dear Reader

---

since the first publication of this book at the beginning of 2020. We've been through it, haven't we? It's been a time of deep unsettling and unrest in many different regards; and we are all grappling as a whole and in our own ways as individuals, with the many overwhelming issues that have been brought into the light. I believe for something to be healed, it must first be seen and acknowledged. So, for me, even though this has been a hard and stressful time; perhaps what might even be described as a dark night of the soul in our world, there is also a lot of hope and goodness to be found. When we are brave enough to step into our inner work, we are then able to contribute in ways that align us with our joy and a deep sense of fulfillment and purpose. When we're able to do this as individuals, as partners, as families, and as communities, we then have the power to transform the world and make it a better place for all. I hope this book can be a touch point of light for you, giving you some tools that can assist you along that path of transformation and beauty-making in your life and in the world.

With Love and Gratitude,
Laura Rain

Dedications

To Moon Child, and all of the many beautiful spiritual misfits that I have had the pleasure of getting to know over the years. Thank you for being muses for this book.

Acknowledgments

I have many people to be grateful for who have supported me in this book-writing journey.

My husband, Michael, who has been my biggest fan. He has encouraged me, challenged me, and unconditionally loved and supported me through the process.

Artist, Victoria Williams Steen, for the cover design and illustration, technology and marketing assistance, and most importantly her friendship, heartfelt wisdom, and generosity of spirit.

Editor, Heidi Bright, for her guidance and assistance with the initial phase of the book.

Author, Tara L. Robinson, for contributing the foreword and for sharing her wisdom that supported me throughout the process.

Author, Mary Ann Henry, for her writer's retreat that sparked and validated the beginning stages of writing the book and my potential as a writer.

Publisher, Robin Surface, for her kind, supportive presence while publishing the book.

Artist, Andee Marley, for the creation of the online downloadable companion to the book, and for her life-saving advice, technical assistance, and fairy magic.

My mom, Donna Martin, and in-laws, Joe and Marti Alford, in helping care for my children. Without their support, the book would probably not be published until 2030.

All my children, who have taught me greater selflessness, love, and patience. These things have served me well in the birthing of this book. My son, Samuel, who gave me the greatest gift of becoming a mother and whose energy was present during much of the writing of the book.

Teachers, Bodhi Avinasha, Pat Sheehan, Gary Woodcox, Richard and Antionette Asimus, Anyaa McAndrew, and the many other counselors, mentors and

Acknowledgements

healers. Without your wisdom and guidance, I surely would have been lost in the ethers forever.

Past partners, friends, and family, who are far too many to name. You have all helped me become who I am today.

May you all be blessed!

Disclaimer

The personal stories of struggle and triumph used as examples throughout the book are a compilation of personal journeys I have witnessed throughout my years of private practice. In order to protect the privacy of all individuals, names have been changed and details have been significantly altered by combining two or three real-life examples to create one illustration.

"We are a way for the universe to know itself.
Some part of our being knows this
is where we came from.
We long to return.
And we can, because the cosmos is also within us.
We're made of star-stuff."

~ Carl Sagan

The Ten Rules for Being Human

- You will receive a body.
- You will be presented with lessons.
- There are no mistakes, only lessons.
- Lessons are repeated until learned.
- Learning does not end.
- "There" is no better than "here."
- Others are only mirrors of you.
- What you make of your life is up to you.
- All the answers lie inside of you.
- You will forget all of this at birth.

~ *If Life is a Game than These are the Rules*
by Cherie Carter-Scott

Table of Contents

Letter to the Reader .... *iii*

Foreword by Tara L. Robinson .... *xxiii*

Introduction
  Spiritual Misfits ....*xxix*

Step 1:   Embrace Who You Are 1

Step 2:   Be Here Now 15

Step 3:   Know You Are Not Alone 27

Step 4:   Let Go of the Past 43

Step 5:   Love Yourself... 55

Step 6:   Experience Pleasure 67

Step 7:   Be One... 79

Step 8:   Align with Your Purpose 89

Afterword:
  The Author's Journey 105

Foreword

by Tara L. Robinson

Dear Reader,

Being a Seeker in this world is not always easy. When we awaken to our divinity and realize we are spiritual beings having a human experience, we realize we need others who understand us more than ever. We need others who will speak our language and hold our hand as we become the heroes and heroines of our own adventures, while simultaneously living seemingly "normal" lives.

As we go about our day to day tasks and work our way through our pragmatic to-do lists, there's an ever-pressing voice in the background prompting us to keep our spiritual eyes wide open to the sacred opportunities present in each moment. We know we are not from here and are only visiting for a short while. That knowing is holy and that knowing makes all the difference.

It turns the mundane into another turn on our sacred path as we engage an epic quest internally. If we pay attention, we are often fortunate enough to receive external clues as to our next assignment. *Not From Here* is one of those points of light. Laura Rain is one of the few who understand this journey and can accompany us on the path, not only holding our hands as a companion, but leading the way with the light of her wisdom.

I met Laura several years ago when she attended a workshop for writers I was hosting. I was instantly drawn to her. Her energy was grounded and infectious. I watched as the group responded to her as such. She was gracious in her communication, yet powerful in her presence. She knew and spoke Truth. I saw then that she had many gifts to offer the world. She is here with a message the world desperately needs.

I was thrilled when she contacted me to celebrate the completion of this book. Yes! The book was finally ready. As I reviewed *Not From Here*, I was pleasantly surprised to see how accessible she had made the content. This is a manual for those who are awake and for those who are awakening. I am impressed by Laura's ability to infuse layers of depth and meaning into sentences and paragraphs structured in an easy-to-read style.

You may not be from here, but you are not alone. May you be blessed by new awareness, new tools, and new hopes as you journey through this beautiful book, which is reaching your hands in perfect timing to meet you exactly where you are on your quest. May you always feel the light shining within and illuminating the path before you. May you always remember you are loved.

Warmly,

Tara L. Robinson
(author *The Ultimate Risk*, Hay House)

*"You are here for a reason.
If you think you're not
I would just say that perhaps you forgot.
A piece of the world that is precious and dear
would surely be missing if you weren't here."*

~Nancy Tillman

INTRODUCTION

Spiritual Misfits

Welcome! Your soul has arrived on planet Earth. Now what? If you find yourself wondering what you are doing here and find yourself longing for home (wherever that might be), believe me, there is hope. You can find a way to be and feel at home here; on Earth, in your body, connected to your soul, to your purpose, and living the life you are meant to live, and enjoying it! Does this seem out of reach from where you are today? I can promise you it is well within your reach. We have all come here for a reason, as part of a divine plan, so let's get to work and find out why you are here and what you came here to do!

If you have felt drawn to pick up this book, you may feel like you belong from somewhere else; a societal or spiritual foreigner. You also may have had past or current experiences of being ostracized for your differences. You might be a spiritual misfit or an outcast for a failure to conform to organized religions, cultural standards, or other societal systems. You may be one of the empaths, highly sensitive or intuitive ones, healers, meditators, animal communicators, or the ones who find deep spiritual meaning in nature. While you may feel judged and alone for being different, deep down inside, you know you have a gift and a purpose for being here. The purpose of this book is to help you embrace who you are and recognize the gifts you have so you may use them to help yourself and others.

In my private practice as a spiritual counselor, I have had the experience of many people coming to me over the years for spiritual guidance and healing believe they are not from here. By saying "here", yes, I mean planet Earth. These people are not crazy or psychotic. They are good-standing members of their families and their communities. They are educated and have professional careers. They are mothers, fathers, teachers, public servants, doctors, nurses, counselors, students, and entrepreneurs. They often find themselves drawn to the helping professions. They also are often interested in the healing and intuitive arts, spirituality, New Age thought, and metaphysics. They are perfectly functioning and intelligent adults, living their lives and appearing to be normal. They have learned how to live within our society and are doing the best they can within it.

In contrast, others may find their way to me because they have not yet learned how to live within our society. They know they are different and have an extremely difficult time functioning. These people often will be battling depression and anxiety or other mental and emotional disorders. They have a challenging time finding guidance that is actually helpful because it tends to lack a holistic and spiritual perspective. Despite the functional differences in these two groups of people, I have found there is a commonality of spiritual crisis and human trauma many of these people have that interferes with their abilities to be really, truly happy here. I endearingly have termed this the "Not from Here" crisis.

These people often have the feeling they were "dropped off" at a wrong location, within biological families in which they don't feel they belong. They often feel they are the "black sheep" of their families or communities. In many instances, they do not want to be here, and have had painful experiences of not fitting in or conforming to the "norm." Although they sense or know they are here for a reason, they typically do not understand what that reason is. Some are aware they are here to help somehow. Some think they are here to learn lessons. Others fear they are here because of a mistake they made, like a form of karmic punishment. Most are extremely empathic and sensitive. Their ability to tolerate violence, cruelty or injustice is minimal and they can find these to be painful. Most are exasperated, feel stuck here, and just want to learn whatever they are supposed to learn in this lifetime so they do not have to come back here and do it all over again. In my experience, the discontent these people feel often comes from feeling cut off or disconnected from the reasons they are here. In other words, they have forgotten their purpose.

If you recognize yourself in these pages, rest assured there is hope. Know that when you remember who you really are and align yourself with your purpose, you will find your life becoming a series of synchronistic events that will lead you to where you need to be next. You will find the connection you are longing for. You will no longer feel alone, cut off from the rest of society. You will begin to release your judgment of this place, other humans, and of yourself, knowing we are all part of a divine plan. More and more, you will find yourself enjoying being here and delighting in the pleasures of having a body. You will begin to see Earth as a beautiful place, filled with magic, wonder, and adventure. And, let's not forget about love. Earthly love in all its expressions is one of the primary reasons we are here and is one of the experiences that makes this world we live in a magical place.

How to Use This Book

Throughout these pages, you will find practical and insightful guidance for finding your freedom to be authentically you in the world and living purposely.

Within each chapter, you will find a series of numbered bullet points that are given as points of awareness for potential thought patterns, feelings, and behaviors that are associated with each topic. As you read through them, please keep in mind there are many shades of gray contained in each one of these bullet points. I invite you to stay away from *black-white, either-or, or always-never* thinking as we humans are so capable of having many polarized thoughts and feelings at the same time; and there are times we might have these thoughts, feelings, and behaviors, and at other times not. As you read, I invite you to be open to the possibilities of *shades of gray, both-and, and sometimes- sometimes not* ideas as a way to broaden and open yourself to the many possibilities of what might be true or not true for you. Remember to hold a space of non-judgment and loving-kindness with any new self-discoveries!

At the end of each chapter, there are a series of journaling exercises and meditations that will help you integrate and put into practice what you have read. You can either read the meditations as they are written or if you prefer to listen to the meditation, you may download a free audio companion from my website: www.holisticspiritualcounseling.com.

Regardless of how you use this book, my hope for you is: You will remember and connect to who you really are and the reasons why you are here. You will heal from any traumatic experiences or disconnections you have experienced. You will discover the personal freedom and empowerment to embark upon your life's purpose. Finally, you will be able to experience all the love, joy, and beauty of being here on this planet at this time in your human form, all the while embracing and accepting yourself, your life, and what you came here to do.

*"True Belonging is the spiritual practice
of believing in and belonging to yourself
so deeply that you can share your most authentic self
with the world and find sacredness in both
being a part of something and standing alone
in the wilderness.
True belonging doesn't require you to change
who you are; it requires you to be who you are."*

~Brene Brown

Embrace
Who You Really Are

"Let the Ego be of service to the Soul."

~ Bodhi Avinasha

One of the ways we humans define ourselves is through our egos. Our egos provide a way for us to tell that we are separate from everything else that exists. The ego is a necessary part of us that has many important duties and functions. On the positive side, it gives us the ability to help ourselves be safe, operate our daily lives, remember and learn from past mistakes, make plans for the future, and accomplish goals.

The ego also can:

1. Keep us stuck in the past or worried about the future.
2. Judge, criticize and sabotage ourselves and others.
3. Compare and make ourselves either better or worse than others.
4. Use fear to control us, keeping us from doing things that are outside our comfort zones.
5. Use our feelings of shame, unworthiness, guilt, and over responsibility to keep us in unhealthy relationships or situations.
6. Control us through old patterns and reactions.
7. Engage in drama.

Let's look at an example:

Nina's father died when she was very young. She was raised by her grieving mother and spent her childhood feeling sad and alone. When she was 17, she met a young man and fell deeply in love. They spent three wonderful years together and were engaged to be married. On the day of Nina's wedding, her fiancé had a change of heart and could not go through with the wedding. On that day, Nina vowed to never love again.

Several years later, she married a man who would be a good provider and father to their future children, but whom she did not love. They had three children together. Nina poured her heart and soul into raising her children but ignored her husband and her marriage. She feared the day when her children would leave to go to college and clung tightly to them, causing them to want to push her away. When her youngest child left the house, she was left alone to face the life she had created with her choices. She judged herself harshly for her mistakes and for her unhappy marriage. She felt weak, stupid, and trapped in the life she had created. In this case, many years of Nina's life had been shaped by her ego's protective response to the abandonment and heartbreak she had experienced as a young woman.

Nina knew she needed help with knowing what to do next in her life. She went on a spiritual and healing inner journey. She discovered how her ego had been trying to protect her from getting hurt again, and realized she no longer needed to protect herself in that way. She forgave herself for her past mistakes and learned to trust herself again.

She found parts of herself that she had buried or forgotten about and learned to love herself again. She faced her fears and let them go. She began to live her life from a place of wholeness. She and her husband began marriage counseling. She realized she could accept the love of this man who had been there for her and learn how to love him as well.

Within this freedom, she embraced the lessons she learned from her life's journey and desired to find a new purpose. She went back to school and became a counselor in a grief center. Today, empowering young women to live life fully and have healthy relationships has become her life's fulfilling and heartfelt endeavor.

For Nina, and probably for most of us, the ego is like an overprotective parent who thinks it knows what is best for us when really, it does not. The ego tries to make us believe we are the roles we play or the labels we have; that our past and our experiences define us; that we are our thoughts, feelings or emotions; that we are the judgments or projections we have about ourselves or others have about us; that we are what we do or what we have. With all this deception, it is no wonder the ego often gets a bad rap in New Age spirituality.

Many belief systems try to kill off the ego as a way to connect with the Divine, but the answer is not to kill the ego. After all, the ego is only doing its best to help us. If we aren't in control of our lives, then somebody's got to be, right? Thank your ego. It's been working hard for you, even if it's not in ways you appreciate. Embrace your ego. You need your ego to complete your purpose. You need your ego's sense of time, strengths and motivations to help you with your purpose here on Earth. Get to know it intimately. Discover how it works. Find its unique gifts. Love your ego as part of yourself. Laugh at your ego and its musings. Lastly, learn how to control your ego and make it work for you.

How do you make the ego work for you? First, learn the difference between when you are operating out of your ego versus when you are operating out of the authentic you. Some might call the authentic self the higher self. It is the part of you that is connected to your soul. Your soul is the part of you that is connected to the Universe or to the Divine / God / All that is / Source / Spirit / Energy, whatever you prefer to call it.

You can tell you are connected to your soul when:

1. You are living in the present moment, trusting in the Divine order. Although you recognize there is a past and a future in this earthly realm, there is no need to worry or have fears about it and you certainly do not need to live there in your mind.

2. You are loving and compassionate with yourself. You are aware of your ego, your thoughts, your experiences, and your feelings, but you know they are not you. They are just part of your experience of being human. You extend this same loving and compassionate energy to others.

3. You know you are connected and one with all that is and there is no need for judgment, criticism, comparison, or separation.

4. You are connected to your intuition and to higher wisdom.
5. You are at peace.
6. There are no emotional triggers.
7. There is no need to engage in drama.

We are able to find our true, authentic selves when the soul and the ego are one, with the soul in control. How do you make the soul and the ego united as one team?

By doing the things that feed the soul and to identify with who you really are; a wise and authentic being, connected to your soul. The most powerful or effective way I'm aware that a person can begin to feel connected is through meditation. Exploring meditation and finding the right technique for you can sometimes be a challenge, but I encourage you to keep trying. Find a technique that helps you begin to still your mind from the chattering voices inside your head. It is in this stillness, that you can begin to feel the presence of who you really are.

After you feel connected to this soul essence inside of you, you can make the distinction between when you are in your soul space versus when you are in your ego space. Your soul can begin to observe and make friends with the ego. From the loving, compassionate witness of your soul space, you can see how the personality traits of your ego and the experiences you have had as a human can be of service to the greater good. From this place of knowing and acknowledging what your ego has to offer, you can let your ego know you are now in control and it must be in partnership with and play a supportive role for you. This can be a journey of integration that can take some time, so be patient and loving with yourself.

How will you know when you are being in your true authentic self, with the soul and the ego working together in service of the higher good?

1. You will love and take care of yourself.

2. You will be able to differentiate between the voice of fear and the voice of intuition.

3. You will live from a place of trust in yourself and in the Divine plan.

4. You will be in your integrity at all times.

5. You will make empowered conscious choices.

6. Your emotional triggers will no longer control you.

7. You will use your energy wisely and live purposely.

Journaling Exercise

One aspect of the ego's role is to judge, criticize, and sabotage yourself. Make a list of all the things you do not like about yourself.

_____
_____
_____
_____
_____
_____
_____
_____
_____
_____
_____

Now, look at each one of these statements. Are these things that you have written really a true reflection of who you are? Most likely, they are not. They most likely are either something you did, a habit you have, or a thought or feeling you have about yourself. Recognize that these beliefs about yourself do not equal who you are and do not serve you. Tell this part of your ego: "Thanks for sharing, but I really am somebody different than these words!"

Affirmation

Close your eyes. Take three deep breaths. Inhale through your nose and exhale through your mouth. Find a tender or sore spot on the left side of your chest; it may feel connected to your heart center. Repeat the following affirmation statement to yourself three times:

"Even though I am human and am not perfect,
I deeply and completely love and accept myself."

When complete, take a deep breath, inhaling through your nose and exhaling out your mouth, and open your eyes. Notice how you feel.

Journaling Exercise:

Make a list of all the things you like about yourself, including any gifts you have.

_____
_____
_____
_____
_____
_____
_____
_____
_____
_____
_____
_____
_____
_____
_____
_____

Look at this list; recognize these are unique expressions of your personality and positive aspects of your ego, which can assist you in being of service in your own way! These are clues that will help put you on track to finding your purpose.

Guided Meditation

Find a comfortable position and close your eyes. Take three long, deep breaths, in through your nose and out through your mouth. Adjust your body until you are completely relaxed and comfortable. Allow your breathing to become calm and steady. Begin to visualize a beautiful universal white light above the crown of your head, connecting you to Divine Energy. As you breathe in, visualize this white light coming down into the crown of your head and down through your body. As you exhale, send the white light out through the soles of your feet. Continue with each inhale to bring in white light, bathing your entire body, and with each exhale, send it out through the soles of your feet and to the earth. Do this at least three times. Now, envision the white light from above-gathering anything and everything that no longer serves you; any negative energy, belief, trauma, emotion or pain you have held. Visualize this white light gathering all of this energy that no longer serves, and exhale it out through the soles of your feet, allowing the earth to use it as compost. Each inhale, you gather more of what no longer serves you in the white light and with each exhale, send it out through the soles of your feet. Do this at least three times. Now, begin to visual-

ize yourself walking in a beautiful place. This place can either be real or imaginary. Take in and breathe in all the sights, sounds, and feelings of this magical place. As you walk, you come to a clearing. In the middle of the clearing, someone is waiting for you. There is no need for fear or worry. This soul radiates nothing but pure love for you. You walk closer and discover that this person or being is an aspect of you; of your higher self. Be with this part of yourself. Take your time.

It is now time to make your way back. Thank this part of yourself for all its wisdom and for your experience. Head through the clearing on to the path you were walking in your beautiful place. Find your room, your body, and your breath. Take a few deep, slow breaths and let them out. Stretch yourself in whatever way feels good to you. Eventually, with another deep breath and gratitude in your heart for this time spent in connection, open your eyes. The meditation is now complete. Feel free to write about anything learned from your experience.

When you embrace who you are and what you are here to do, you will find the world a more comfortable place to call home, even if it's just for this lifetime.

Be Here Now

"Be Love. Be Here. Be Now."

~ Ram Dass

Spiritual misfits can often have a difficult time being grounded and connected to the earth and living life from a place of trust. What are the warning signs of a person not being connected to this time and place?

They often:

1. Run late; lack in time management skills.

2. Are constantly in their heads thinking about the past or future.

3. Distrust themselves and others.
4. Have anxiety, fears, or phobias.
5. Often experience "space cadette" moments.
6. Have issues with money, food, body image, and / or sex.
7. Experience physical pain or issues in their legs, feet, lower back, and hips, including elimination and reproductive areas.

Part of the reason people are disconnected is that they tend to feel comfortable and safe when they are not present in their bodies. These people can often seem "flighty" or be described as "having their heads in the clouds." If a person has had the experience of being present and grounded, they will usually recognize when they are not. Sometimes, though, if they have not experienced what it is like to be present and in their bodies, they simply do not know what it means or feels like. They may think they are grounded when they really are not.

When people are spiritually connected but ungrounded, they may intuitively know things and have access to higher wisdom, yet they usually are unable to bring that wisdom down to the earthly realm and into their bodies. They may have problems with healing from traumas because they are more interested in understanding them rather than healing, which requires an in-the-body experience. They may have an interest in focusing all on the light or the positive and be unwilling to face the shadow or the dark sides of themselves and be averse to feeling the pain of their own experiences. They may also be highly intelligent, yet lack emotional intelligence, and be controlled by their emotional reactions.

These people often gravitate toward "spiritual bypasses," which are spiritual teachings that take people out of their bodies and into the higher realms of consciousness. Taking people out of their bodies without first dealing with their physical, mental and emotional issues can create a bigger disconnect between the soul and the ego and the soul and the body. If a person has not dealt with issues around money, their body, traumas, or other earthly matters, then no matter how high they might fly, those matters will pull them crashing back down until they are willing to face them and do something about them.

Let's look at an example:

Mary spent years working on herself and recovering from childhood abuse inflicted by her alcoholic father who often became violent when drunk. Mary is a full-time nurse, practices daily meditation and prayer, is part of her church community, and has a part-time energy healing practice. Mary is often exhausted and angry with her body that is too large for her frame. She has experienced several failed attempts at conquering her sugar addiction and sticking with an exercise plan. Mary dreams of quitting her nursing job and making a living through her healing work, yet she doesn't believe she can afford to.

Even though she is constantly exhausted and worried about money, she gives her healing services away for free or for a discount to people she feels really need her and can't afford to pay her rate. She puts her faith in God that someday she will be able to live the life of her dreams when she retires. Mary is an example of a spiritual and faithful being who is being pulled down by her unresolved issues that are manifesting in lack of financial abundance, weight gain, codependence (making other people's needs more important than her own), and escapism.

Mary got fed up with her exhaustion, money, and weight problems; she knew she needed a change. She sought out body-centered movement therapy to help her drop her spiritual awareness down into her body and to heal from the emotional and physical traumas she still was carrying in the tissues of her body. Once she healed on a mind, body, spirit level, she was able to put into practice many of the spiritual principles she had long understood, and follow the advice she had often given to others.

She stopped giving away her services, learned to value herself, and was able to cut her sugar addiction. She also made time for self-care and exercise, which helped her lose the extra weight, which she had been carrying around her like a protective cocoon. She was able to put together a financially responsible business plan for her early retirement and her transition into her life's purpose of doing healing work.

Today, she continues working part-time as a nurse, doing the energy healing work she loves, takes care of herself well, and has found additional life purpose and joy assisting at self-care retreats and workshops.

We don't have to leave our bodies or escape into dreams of the future to find bliss or happiness. Bliss is available right here, right now. Once we decide to be present and create happiness now, we can clear through the issues that are preventing us from having the fulfilling experiences we want, including finding and completing our purposes here.

How do you know when you are being present and grounded in your life?

1. You will live in the moment. Being present will become a natural state of being.

2. You will spend less time spinning in the continual thoughts and musings of the mind. You will live more in your body, noticing and following the subtle, intuitive, and knowing language of your body.

3. You will live in a place of trust with yourself, others, and the Divine. Trust will be innate until there is a real reason or intuition to distrust another person or situation. You will trust yourself to know the difference.

4. You will know how to witness or observe fear and be able to distinguish between fear and intuition.

5. You will feel drawn to spend more time being one with nature and feel a connection with the earth.

6. You will live in abundance and gratitude, viewing the world as a place of plenty rather than lack.

7. You will be in acceptance of yourself and your life. Finding happiness in the now.

Journaling Exercise

How is fear playing a role in your life? Complete the following sentences:

I am afraid of:

_____
_____
_____
_____
_____
_____

I worry about:

_____
_____
_____
_____
_____
_____

I avoid living my life by:

_____
_____
_____
_____
_____
_____

Take a look at these lists. Pick out your top three fears, worries, or avoidance techniques. Use the following affirmation to work through your top picks.

Affirmation

Close your eyes. Take three deep breaths. Inhale through your nose and exhale through your mouth. Find a tender or sore spot on the left side of your chest that may feel connected to your heart center. Repeat the following affirmation statement to yourself three times:

"Even though I'm afraid
(fill in the fear, worry, etc.),
I deeply and completely let it go and trust
(fill in what you want to find your trust in—
God, yourself, the divine plan for your life, etc.)."

When complete, take a deep breath, inhaling through your nose and exhaling out your mouth. Open your eyes. Notice how you feel.

Journaling Exercise:

Make a list of possibilities by completing the following sentence:

If I were not in fear, I would

_____
_____
_____
_____
_____
_____
_____
_____
_____
_____

Look at this list. Become aware of how your fears may have been in control. Choose one item on your list and choose to do it, and then another. Soon, you will come to realize you are not allowing your fears to control your life. You will realize you are living out of a place of empowered trust, enjoying your life, being more grounded, and allowing your actions and behaviors to reflect more authentically who you are and what you came here to do.

Guided Meditation

Find a comfortable position and close your eyes. Take three long, deep breaths, in through your nose and out through your mouth. Adjust your body until you are completely relaxed and comfortable. Allow your breathing to become calm and steady. Begin to visualize a beautiful glowing gold light above the crown of your head. This light represents calm, peace, and higher wisdom. As you inhale, visualize this golden light coming in through the crown of your head and making its way all the way down your body. As you exhale, send this light out through your feet. With each inhale, you draw more golden light from above, bathing your entire body. Each exhale, you send it out through your feet. Continue.

Now, allow yourself to rest your awareness at the soles of your feet. Imagine here a luminous silver light. This light represents nurturing and supportive Mother Earth energy. As you inhale, draw this vibrant silver light up through the soles of your feet, and all the way up through your entire body. As you exhale, send this energy out through the crown of your head, showering your entire energy field like a fountain and letting it descend back down to the Earth. With each inhale you draw more supportive, grounding energy from the Earth all the way up your body. With each exhale, you send this energy out through the crown of your head, bathing your body and your energy field all the way back down to the Earth. Continue at your own pace for a minimum of three cycles of breath.

Release the meditation and notice how you feel. Become aware of the energy that supports you. Become aware of your body and the way it is supported by the chair or the floor. Notice your breath. Take a few deep, slow breaths and let them out. Stretch yourself in whatever way feels good to you. Eventually, with another deep breath, feel gratitude in your heart for this moment of connection with earth energy. Open your eyes. The meditation is now complete. Feel free to journal about anything learned from your experience.

Once we come into acceptance that we are here for a reason and we allow ourselves to be here in this moment at this time, we open ourselves to the extraordinary experience and magic of being.

Know You Are Not Alone

"We have all known the long loneliness and we have learned that the only solution is love and that love comes with community."

~ Dorothy Day

Many spiritual misfits feel they are alone for good reason. As children, most have had difficult experiences of not fitting in with their peers, their families, or their communities. Often these people feel they were "dropped off" at the wrong location as they belong somewhere else. This feeling of seclusion can extend well into adulthood. I have found there are two different types of reactions people have to this feeling of isolation that can take them further into isolation. One response a person may have is to embrace and take pride in being separate and misunderstood. These people will tend to expound upon their differences and find their identity in their uniqueness, which in and of itself is great, but in an unhealthy expression can include:

1. Angry self-expression, with the intention of being rebellious or shocking to others or to normal societal standards.

2. Judgmental attitudes toward organizations, including religious, governmental, and big corporations, and toward any persons connected with them.

3. Flippant or uncaring attitudes.

Let's look at an example:

Harry grew up in a small town. He did not do well in school because he had a different learning style than what he was being taught. He described school and all of his teachers as "stupid." He also had a difficult time fitting in with other kids because he didn't care about the same things they did. His parents did not understand him and would often shun him for not being like his brother, who did well in school and was popular with his peers. Harry spent a significant amount of his time alone in his room, playing guitar and gaming. The friends he made online were his primary social connections.

As he became a teenager, he met a group of kids who were starting a band and were in need of a guitar player. This was a perfect opportunity for him to get to play and have a group of friends. Through his longing to fit in, however, he started drinking, vaping, and experimenting with drugs. As Harry became an adult, he had no interest in becoming part of the "Man," as he liked to call it, but did not know what else to do with his life. He lived with his parents and spent most of his days high, gaming, and avoiding living his life.

One night, Harry had an out-of-body experience while under the influence of a psychedelic drug. This trip took him into the void and into the deepest recesses of his mind, where he experienced oneness with all that is. When he came back from the trip, he began to seek out more mind-expanding experiences. He learned he could have deeply spiritual experiences of oneness through shamanic ceremonies, powerful breathwork, and meditation exercises. He gave up the need or desire for external substances to fulfill his desire for a connection to something deeper. He stopped the avoidance techniques he was using to not live his life and began really living. He enrolled in a computer science program, did well, and got a job he enjoys and does well. He lives on his own and takes responsibility for his life. He still enjoys gaming, hanging with his friends, and being part of the band, but no longer feels the need to use drugs. He continues exploring spiritual practices and has found a spiritual like-minded community that meditates together once a week.

Harry had allowed his ego to express itself by judging others and creating a wall of separation between himself and the rest of the world. This was his way of feeling safe. He now accepts and embraces who he truly is, so he can enjoy his life and have a healthy connection with others.

The second type of reaction a person may have to isolation is to experience a deep longing to be understood and to fit in, yet end up feeling deeply hurt, rejected and develop a crippling fear of judgment. These people will often respond to this fear of rejection and judgment by developing people-pleasing and chameleon-like behaviors to shapeshift into whatever they sense another person or group wants them to be.

Symptoms of people who experience this kind of behavior include:

1. Lack of personal opinions, often responding with "I don't know" when asked a question of what to do or how they feel about something. They often will default to what someone else thinks or wants to do.

2. Lack of personal boundaries, allowing others' needs and wants to be more important

than their own. This can leave them feeling used by others.

3. Hiding or trying to fit in. They may look and act conventional or mainstream, yet they feel like they carry a secret inside that haunts them; that if people found out who they Really Are, that they will not be liked.

4. Super Man/Clark Kent Syndrome, which is the label I lovingly use to describe when a person chooses to stay hidden, taking pride in knowing they are different and feeling they are secretly better than others.

Let's look at an example: Marjory was an incredibly sensitive and empathic child. She had a deep connection to Mother Earth and animals. She sensed she was important and was part of a bigger plan, and knew she had a purpose in being here.

As Marjory became school age and had more interactions with peers, she realized she was different from others. Her peers did not seem to think she was important at all. In fact, they rejected her for being different. Marjory ended up feeling ashamed of who she was. She decided it would be less painful to try and fit in, so she spent most of her childhood trying to be popular with her peers and doing whatever she could to fit in with the crowd. She often found herself in situations that were uncomfortable, but she was afraid to speak up. Her "friends" were often mean to her and used her for their benefit. She often felt invisible and hid how she was feeling. She was most comfortable being herself with her animals, who were her best friends.

As an adult, Marjory performed the expected. She went to college, got a job, got married, and had a family. On the outside, Marjory appeared to have a perfectly normal existence, yet on the inside, Marjory felt like something was missing. She knew she was unhappy, but didn't know why. That young girl who knew her importance had been long forgotten. Marjory knew she didn't feel right and needed to do something about it. She began by reading some self-help books and journaling. During this process, she realized she didn't know who she was. She became aware of how crippling her fear was of being rejected and judged because she was different. Marjory embarked upon a long journey of self-exploration. She discovered things about herself she had forgotten. This has led her to have the experiences she desires and has stopped caring what others may think. She gives herself permission to be wrong and to make mistakes. She laughs more, loves more, and is having fun exploring who she really is. She takes long walks in the woods, sits by rivers, journals, sings, and is remembering herself as that young girl who knew of her importance. She now is part of a neighborhood organization that works to keep parks beautiful and free of litter. She feels content, happy and at peace with herself and her life.

Similar to many people that have had this experience of division, the answers both Harry and Marjory discovered were to be authentically who they were within the fabric of the whole. Through this alignment and discovery within themselves, they were able to more easily see where they fit in and where they could find purposeful and meaningful endeavors for themselves. When we are able to let go of our fear and be real with ourselves and others, we can more easily align with the people and places that we can feel a sense of community and belong in.

Like Harry and Marjory experienced, even if you are currently feeling separate and judged, it's highly likely that you are part of a greater plan. There exists a network of other sensitive souls like yourself who

Know You Are Not Alone

are all here for a reason. By Being Who You Are, Where You Are, you have the ability to break patterns of dysfunction in yourself. This healing of the self has the power to initiate change and for the greater good of our families, communities, and in our world.

By being you and allowing others to see you in your light, you give others permission to shine their own lights. No one has to be alone. A wonderful part of being human is connecting with others and enjoying relationships. Finding a community of like-minded people is part of what makes us happy and feel fulfilled.

What does it look like to be connected and a part of the whole?

1. You love and accept yourself and others for their differences.
2. You no longer feel inferior or superior. You sense the equality in all people.
3. You have authentic relationships with others.
4. You let yourself be seen by others, not needing to live in a protective shell.
5. You do not allow fear of judgment from others to control you.
6. You are a part of a community.
7. You let your light shine!

Journaling Exercise

Make a list of the ways and reasons you keep yourself separate from others by completing the following sentences.

The ways in which I keep myself separate are:

_____
_____
_____
_____
_____
_____
_____
_____

I keep myself separate because:

_____
_____
_____
_____
_____
_____
_____
_____

One of the best ways you can find your community, spiritual tribe, friendships, or even a romantic partner is to seek out opportunities to meet others who are aligned with your interests.

Complete the sentence:

The things I enjoy doing, wish I could do, or the things that interest me are:

_____
_____
_____
_____
_____
_____
_____
_____
_____
_____
_____
_____
_____
_____
_____
_____
_____
_____
_____
_____
_____
_____
_____
_____
_____
_____

Affirmation

Close your eyes. Take three deep breaths. Inhale through your nose and exhale through your mouth. Find a tender or sore spot on the left side of your chest, which may feel connected to your heart center. Repeat the following affirmation statement to yourself three times:

> "Even though I feel like I am alone,
> I deeply and completely love and accept myself
> and allow myself to feel connected."

When complete, take a deep breath, inhaling through your nose and exhaling out your mouth. Open your eyes. Notice how you feel.

Guided Meditation:

Find a comfortable position and close your eyes. Take three long, deep breaths, in through your nose and out through your mouth. Adjust your body until you are completely relaxed and comfortable. Allow your breathing to become calm and steady. Begin to visualize a beautiful glowing gold light above the crown of your head. This light represents calmness, peace, and higher wisdom. As you inhale, visualize this golden light coming in through the crown of your head and making its way all the way down your body. As you exhale, send this light out through your feet. With each inhale, you draw more golden light from above, bathing your entire body. With each exhale, you send it out through your feet. Continue.

Now, allow yourself to rest your awareness at the soles of your feet. Imagine here a luminous silver light. This light represents nurturing and supportive Mother Earth energy. As you inhale, draw this vibrant silver light up through the soles of your feet, and all the way up through your entire body. As you exhale, send this energy out through the crown of your head. Bathe your entire energy field with it and let it flow back down to the Earth.

With each inhale you draw more supportive, grounding energy from the Earth all the way up your body. With each exhale, send this energy out through the crown of your head, bathing your body and your energy field all the way back down to the Earth. Now imagine with every breath that you are simultaneously drawing energy from both places, above and below. These energies begin to merge and dance at your heart. Imagine now that this energy forms a perfect white light. Now with each exhale, you imagine that light growing bigger, expanding into every cell of your body.

Expanding even more quickly now, you imagine that light growing and expanding into your energy field, including all the space that surrounds you. Soon, the white light expands beyond your energy field. It begins to travel, connecting you with the white light of all the other beautiful souls on the planet who also are on this spiritual journey with you. Feel a sense of connection with them. Know that all of you working together are helping to make this world a better place with your love. Allow your heart to be open to this community of souls that you are a part of. Allow yourself to feel that connectedness and know that you are part of a bigger plan. When you are ready, keeping this feeling of connection with you, begin to breathe deeply again. Wriggle your fingers and toes and stretch in any way that feels comfortable to you. When you are ready, open your eyes.

When we no longer spend our energy adapting ourselves to either fit in or not fit in, we can celebrate our own uniqueness. From that space, we allow ourselves and others to shine!

Let Go of the Past

*"Living in the moment means letting go of the past
and not waiting for the future.
It means living your life consciously,
aware that each moment you breathe is a gift."*

~ Oprah Winfrey

The ego will use past experiences to define itself and even label itself. "I am a survivor" is one example of a label. This function of the ego is necessary. We are meant to learn from our experiences and grow from them. They are a part of the fabric of our existence and we would not be who we are without them. Often people will relive their past experiences repeatedly in their minds. Sometimes people do this as a way to try and understand why something happened. What is the larger or bigger picture? Sometimes, this is revealed. Other times, it is not.

If we can understand why something happened, we can often make peace with an event or situation. Yet what happens if we do not see the bigger picture or the reason why a situation has occurred? Do we hold on to it? Mull it over? Beat ourselves up over it? Refuse to forgive ourselves or others? Live in fear of the past repeating itself? Define ourselves by our wounds? None of this sounds like an appealing way to live, yet this is often what we do. We can become trapped by our thoughts and emotions connected to the past. We allow our personal histories to control us, letting them define who we are and shape our future.

How do we know if we are living in our past?

1. Our thoughts continuously gravitate to past events.

2. We protect ourselves from situations or people that remind us of something in our past.

3. We harbor strong emotions related to the past as if it were happening in the present.

4. We are constantly watching out for dangerous situations out of fear of getting hurt again.

5. We have a difficult time letting a person or situation go.

6. We are unable to accept or forgive.

7. We identify with labels based on experience. Examples might include victim, addict, failure.

Let's look at an example:

Mark is an alcoholic, yet he has been sober for 30 years. He tells himself every day that he is an addict, so he will never forget. Every day he makes amends for all the wrongdoing he did while he was drinking. He feels guilty and mourns the loss of his family and friends during his years of drinking. Although he has done a tremendous amount of personal growth work to get sober, he fears he could relapse and doesn't trust himself to be in close relationships outside of his support groups that affirm him in his story. He spends most of his days feeling lonely and struggles with depression. He has found sobriety, and is fortunately supported in it, yet he has not discovered how to truly live and thrive sober.

When Mark found out he was going to be a grandparent, he had not spoken to his son in fifteen years. Despite his fear of being rejected, he reached out to his son. His son was reluctant at first, yet soon opened to the idea of getting to know his father again. Mark was given the gift of a second chance, the opportunity to have a relationship with his son and become family once again. This one act of courage, vulnerability, and forgiveness by both Mark and his son helped Mark

Let Go of the Past

discover that he had a life worth living. He decided his time and energy would be better spent focusing on the present and on creating a new life for himself rather than dwelling on the mistakes of his past. Through the nature of this healing relationship with his son and new-found family, Mark was able to trust himself again to have healthy relationships with others. He decided to buy a boat and join a sailing club. He learned to scuba dive, all which had been life-long dreams. He eventually met a woman who became a trusted friend and companion. He is now able to see himself and his goodness through her eyes and the eyes of his grandchild. Although he will never forget his life of addiction, he finds himself thinking about it less and less. He has found happiness by creating his life anew.

How do we let go of the past and not let our previous experiences define us? We learn from them, grow healthier, and no longer identify with them. Freedom from the past comes from understanding and truly knowing that all of the experiences we have had helped make us who we are today. They are part of the fabric of our being, yet they are not us. We can live with the memories of our experiences, yet we do not need to live with all the related feelings or wounds. We can live in acceptance of what has been and go on with the art of living in the present moment.

If we are unable to let go of a situation, we must find out how holding onto it is serving us. We must be getting some benefit, or we would be letting it go. Once we discover how holding on is serving us, we can establish whether our grasping serves our highest and best good. Perhaps it is. Perhaps there is something we still need to learn from it. Perhaps it is not. Perhaps it is an operation of the ego's defense system as a way of protecting ourselves. Once we discover our true motivations for not being able to let go, we are more fully able to process the situation, so we are better able to let go in a way that is honoring to ourselves, others, and the experience.

How does it look like to live free from the past? When you recall a person, situation, or event:

1. You feel neutral, compassionate, or even grateful for the experience.

2. There are no negative thoughts.

3. There are no emotional triggers.

Let Go of the Past

4. There are no painful places of holding in the body. (*For example, you do not feel a pain in the gut or in the heart when you think of someone or a situation in the past.*)

5. You have genuine feelings of goodness to come to others.

6. You feel at peace.

7. Love is present.

Journaling Exercise

Formula for letting go:

1. Complete the sentences:

The thing from my past that most controls me is:
___
___
___
___
___
___
___

How that shows up in my life is:
___
___
___
___
___
___
___

What I need to do to let go is:
___
___
___
___
___
___
___

2. Write a letter to either yourself or the person involved in the situation. Say what you need to say. Think of it as a purging that no one else will ever read. Journal what you have learned from the situation and see if you can find at least one gratitude for it.

3. Burn or tear up the letter and release yourself, the other persons involved, and the situation. Include an affirmation statement such as: "I forgive and release myself (and another, if appropriate) from this situation."

   Example: I forgive myself and my ex-husband for not having the tools to know how to make our marriage work. I release myself and him from the pain, shame, and guilt of the divorce.

4. Pay attention to bodily sensations that might arise. Notice if there are any areas speaking to you in the form of pain or energy. Bring your awareness to that area of your body and release the energy that may be present. You can do this by imagining yourself breathing deeply into that area of the body and releasing the breath and energy of the situation out through your mouth. Notice how you feel.

Affirmation

"I give myself permission to let go of the past and live in the present."

One of the illusions people have about forgiveness is a belief that if they forgive themselves others for wrongdoing, it somehow sends the message that the behavior was okay or it opens the door for the behavior to happen again. The act of forgiveness does not mean that the behavior or situation is okay. It very well may not be okay. An example of this may be in the form of some kind of atrocity that has happened to you or a loved one. Forgiveness of the person that committed this act is not a way of "letting this person off the hook" or saying this person does not need to make amends for what he or she has done. What it does mean is that you are no longer willing to hold on to anger or resentment in your own mind or body. You are not going to allow this act to control you or affect you negatively any longer. By forgiving, you release this energy within yourself. You free yourself.

Guided Meditation:

Find a comfortable position and close your eyes. Take three long, deep breaths, in through your nose and out through your mouth. Adjust your body until you are completely relaxed and comfortable. Allow your breathing to become calm and steady. Begin to visualize a beautiful glowing gold light above the crown of your head. This light represents calm, peace, and healing.

As you inhale, visualize this golden light coming in through the crown of your head and making its way all the way down your body. As you allow this breath and energy to move through your body, feel your body radiate with its warm, healing light. In this space, become aware of anything you are holding on to that no longer serves you. Anything that you are ready and willing to let go of. It can be showing up for you as a memory or a situation or as pain in the body. Become aware of the pain you are holding or of the experience that is still causing pain.

Become aware of the people involved or of a situation (including yourself, if it's yourself or something you have done that needs to be released). Now that you have this in your awareness, begin to surround this awareness with the white light, creating a bubble around the experience. With each exhale, imagine that you are letting go of each bubble that you have created and all that is inside this bubble. Release this from your body with a feeling of gratitude for whatever you have learned from the experience. Willingly let go. Once you have finished, feel free to relax all efforts and notice how you feel.

When we let go of whatever no longer serves us, we are ultimately loving ourselves and choosing to make ourselves more important than the experience we are holding on to.

Love Yourself

*"Love yourself first
and everything else falls into line."*

~ Lucille Ball

Loving oneself can sometimes be a foreign concept to people, an idea that has not been given much thought. Often people will respond to the question "Do you love yourself?" with "I don't know, I haven't really ever thought about it." In our society, we are often taught at a young age to not be selfish and to put others' needs above our own. Sometimes, loving oneself can be mistaken with being selfish. Putting ourselves first or taking care of ourselves can be considered self-indulgent. There can be confusion about what loving oneself means or how one can practice or engage in loving acts of kindness toward themselves.

Spiritual misfits can be especially prone to not loving themselves and being hard on themselves. Knowing they are spiritual beings can lead to expectations of perfection of themselves. They can have difficulty accepting themselves as human beings who make mistakes and still are lovable. Since spiritual misfits also tend to be sensitive or empathic beings, they can also take on the disapproval or judgment of others and believe these criticisms to be a truth about themselves.

What are the symptoms of people who do not love themselves?

1. Their self-worth and value are based on what they do rather than who they are.

2. The feeling of not being good enough is ever-present.

3. They strive for perfection and are critical and judgmental of themselves when they fall short.

4. They are hypersensitive to criticism or judgment from others.

5. They seek others' love and approval as a way to help them feel they are okay.

6. They do not take care of themselves or they take part in self-sabotaging behaviors.

7. They treat their needs and wants as unimportant.

8. They live in fear and make fear-based decisions.

Let's look at an example:

Dan grew up in a farming community. His religious ubringing taught him that he was inherently bad and to fear God. From a very young age, he received many messages that a man's value or worth was based on how much money he made, how he provided for his family, and how hard he worked on the farm. There was not much money, and anything Dan wanted to do or have was of little to no importance to his family members, who were focused on survival. Dan secretly found pleasure in dressing in his sister's clothes and dreamed of one day becoming an actor and performing on stage. He found himself being much more attracted to young men than young women at his school. Dan was terrified of anyone knowing. He feared he would be punished by God and shunned by his family and community, so he kept it a secret.

He was so adept at keeping it a secret and living a façade, that he eventually believed the façade to be true and kept the truth of who he was hidden, even from himself. Having buried this part of himself, Dan followed his family's footsteps, did what was expected of him, married his high school sweetheart, had a family, and eventually took over the struggling family farm. Dan became severely depressed and felt like a failure in every area of his life. Although he loved his wife and his family, he struggled to be present with them because he felt he had failed them. His wife wanted to have more intimacy, but Dan had no sex drive and was unable to be intimate. Dan felt lonely, confused, sad, and dead inside. He knew he needed to get help and sought out counseling.

In counseling, he rediscovered and remembered the boyhood dream he had of being an actor on stage. He also allowed himself to remember being more attracted to men than women as a young adult. He eventually admitted to himself that he thought it was possible that he was gay and that he had no attraction for women.

Through remembrance of this denied part of himself, Dan began to flourish. Although he chose to not act upon his remembrances, the act of acknowledging who he is on a deep level brought nourishment and healing to his soul. He began to accept himself for who he was and began to love himself. He was then able to be more present with his wife and children. He no longer felt like a failure.

As he began to love himself, he realized how much of his life he had spent trying to live up to an expectation of worth that had been set up in his childhood and really had nothing to do with him or his desires for his life. He was no longer willing to live a life that did not bring him joy. He decided to sell the farm and move his family into the city where he could begin to explore the arts and the theater. He found a job that didn't get his hands dirty and wasn't hard on his body. He tried an acting class at a community college.

His new-found happiness has made him a more present and loving husband and father. Even though he is still unable to be physically intimate with his wife, they have settled into an agreement that it is okay for now. Although he does not know where his journey will ultimately take him with his new self-realizations, he is happy to be living life one day at a time and exploring a part of himself that he had denied all those years. He is at peace with himself and with his life.

In our society, it is commonplace to ask the question, "What do you do?" and we often ask our children, "What do you want to be when you grow up?" Much of our systemic and educational values are placed on what we do rather than who we are.

Love Yourself

Wouldn't it be wonderful to live in a world where we ask the question, "Who are you?" rather than "What do you do?" Isn't it time we ask ourselves and others, "Who do you want to be?" or "What kind of person are you?" It is time we teach ourselves and our children that who we are is enough. We do not have to do anything to prove our worth.

We are worthy already, just as we are. We are lovable, just as we are. There is nothing to prove. When we love ourselves, we automatically love others as well. When we do not judge ourselves, we automatically do not judge others. When we are compassionate with ourselves, we are compassionate with those around us.

When we love ourselves, we give ourselves permission to follow our joy. Joy is a state of being and our birthright. When we follow our joy, we give others permission to do the same. When we have love in our hearts and we follow our joy, the extensions of that energy have the potential to create a more loving, accepting and joyful world. When we have love in our hearts, we automatically are led to be of service to others in ways that bring ourselves and others gifts. We align with our hearts' purposes.

What are the attributes of self-love?

1. You will take care of and nurture yourself.

2. You will take responsibility for your life.

3. You will make your needs and wants a priority.

4. You will do the work you enjoy.

5. You will be of service to others, helping to make the world a better place.

6. You will be simultaneously in your personal power and have humility.

7. You will be kind, compassionate, and loving.

8. You will make love-based decisions.

Journaling Exercise:

Complete the following sentences on love, joy and self care.

I am worthy because:

_____
_____
_____
_____
_____
_____

I am lovable because:

_____
_____
_____
_____
_____
_____

The things that bring me the most joy are:

_____
_____
_____
_____
_____
_____

If I were more loving towards myself I would:

_____
_____
_____
_____
_____
_____

The way I can be nurturing and taking care of myself is:

_____
_____
_____
_____
_____
_____

Affirmation

"I am worthy.

I am beautiful.

I am lovable just as I am."

Bonus Exercise!

Find a mirror. Gaze deeply into your own eyes. Tell yourself repeatedly for at least three minutes, "I love you." Let it sink in.

Guided Meditation

Find a comfortable position and close your eyes. Take three long, deep breaths, in through your nose and out through your mouth. Adjust your body until you are completely relaxed and comfortable. Allow your breathing to become calm and steady. Begin to bring awareness to the palm of your left hand. Imagine a pink warm light radiating there. This energy represents the energy of unconditional self-love. Now, as you inhale, imagine that you are drawing up this energy through your left arm and into the center of your chest, the home of your heart center. Hold the energy here during a pause between the inhale and the exhale.

As you exhale, send the energy down the right arm, into the right palm of the hand. As you inhale, bring the energy back up the right arm and into the heart center. Pause. As you exhale, send the energy down the left arm and into the left palm. Continue sending this energy back and forth. Pause each time at the heart center between the inhale and the exhale. Take your time. When you are ready, feel free to let go of the meditation and focus your awareness on your heart center. You can even bring your hands to the center of your chest if you'd like. Here, with every breath, know that you have an opportunity to breathe in love and breathe out love. When you are ready, open your eyes.

Where there is love, there is no fear. Where there is love, there is no judgment. Where there is love, there is peace.

Experience Pleasure

"I think we need to teach pleasure. What beautiful touch means. What reciprocity means. What being connected and what intimacy means."

~ Eve Ensler

As we found in Chapter two, spiritual misfits may have a difficult time being grounded. This can be directly linked to their abilities to experience awareness and consciousness within their own bodies. When they are not in their bodies, they are not able to fully feel physical pleasures. There are many reasons spiritual misfits may not feel comfortable living in their bodies. For example, they may be avoiding physical pain. They may also be shying away from the shame that can arise from experiencing a pleasure.

In our society, guilty pleasures go hand-in-hand. Why does pleasure need to be associated with guilt? Guilt is a feeling we have when we have done something wrong or that is not in alignment with our integrity. Having and feeling pleasure is our natural way of being. Have you ever watched a baby have sensory experiences for the first time? They indulge in their exuberant eating, in gazing into a loved one's eyes, in touch, in being held, in taking a bath and feeling the water on their skin. There is so much fun to be had from living a body! Our bodies are made to feel and humans need loving, safe touch to thrive.

Our sensory receptors that are responsible for pleasure also are responsible for sensations of pain. Therefore, pain and pleasure can be intrinsically linked within us. When we avoid pain, we avoid pleasure. We cannot be open to pleasure without also being open to pain. We are either open or we are not. If we are shut down from painful experiences of the past, we are unable to feel the joyful, pleasurable experiences of the moment. Being comfortable and at home in our bodies allows us to be open to blissful experiences. There is no shame in enjoyment. Indulging our bodies and our senses is a gift we can give ourselves, whether that is in the form of a luxurious dinner, making love, or watching a beautiful sunset. There are many ecstatic experiences to be enjoyed here on Earth.

What are some symptoms of a person who is not open to pleasure?

1. The feeling of not being comfortable with the body.

2. Having feelings of shame associated with the body and / or sexuality.

3. Being rigid and holding tightness in the body.

4. Not knowing what brings one pleasure.

5. Not being able to communicate what brings pleasure.

6. The feeling that the body is for someone else's pleasure and not your own.

7. Being disconnected from nature.

It's not easy for some spiritual misfits to accept pleasure. Let's look at an example:

Lisa was sexually abused as a child. This experience left her feeling ungrounded and disconnected from her body. As she grew into a young woman and became sexually active, she felt numb and disconnected during sexual encounters. Often, she would check out of her mind and body during sex and later could not remember what had happened during the act.

For Lisa, sex was about her partner's pleasure, never her own. When asked by her partner what he could do to please her, she did not know what to say. Often, she would fake her orgasm and hide her disconnect by doing what she thought would bring him pleasure so he would love her and not leave her. She had never experienced an orgasm and felt like something was wrong with her. After sex, she felt ashamed, dirty, guilty, and confused. She knew she should not feel this way and wanted something different from her sexual experiences.

Lisa started reading books on women and sexuality, ranging from how to heal from childhood sexual abuse to how to have an orgasm. She put into practice

Experience Pleasure

---

the techniques suggested in the books and went on a healing journey. She began a conscious masturbation practice that helped her get in touch with her body. She worked through the pain that was being held in the tissues of her body. By being willing to work with her pain body, she discovered her pleasure body and began having orgasms and sexual pleasures. She was able to communicate with her partner what she desired. She sought out sacred sex and tantric therapies to further her exploration. It was here she found her sweet spot and continued her journey into healing the spiritual/sexual split and body shame. She opened her heart to be fully present, experiencing the joy of life's pleasures.

In this example, Lisa was disconnected from her body because of her childhood abuse. This is a great example of how leaving one's body and not being willing to feel pain disconnects the person from being able to feel pleasure. When we are not present in our bodies or in the moment, we cannot fully experience what life on Earth or what having a body has to offer. How do we move from a place of disconnect with our bodies to a place of full connection and openness to joyful experiences with the body?

First, we must discover and heal whatever is keeping us from being present and living fully in our bodies, whether this arises from an experience like Lisa's or because we have been taught that giving in to the pleasures of our bodies is sinful or bad. Once we become present, we must be willing to risk and experiment with what brings us pleasure. We must honor ourselves and do what feels good. If we feel pain, we must witness it with awareness and know that our ability to feel pain equals our ability to feel pleasure. We must connect with nature and appreciate her beauty. We must be fully present, loving our bodies as part of ourselves.

What will be your attributes when you are open to pleasure?

1. Your body is relaxed.

2. Your mind is present.

3. Your heart is open.

4. Your soul is at peace.

5. You experience no shame or guilt. Only love.

Experience Pleasure

---

6. You have the freedom to experience without judgment.

7. Your body's needs and desires are important and you meet them.

You were given this body for a reason. Now go out and enjoy it! Marvel at what it can do for you. You're worth it!

Journaling Exercise

Complete the following sentences:

If I were fully living within my body, I would:

_____
_____
_____
_____
_____
_____

The things that keep me from being fully present within my body are:

_____
_____
_____
_____
_____
_____

I feel guilt or shame about:

_____
_____
_____
_____
_____
_____

Something I have wanted to experience yet haven't let myself is:

_____
_____
_____
_____
_____
_____

The things I love about my body are:

_____
_____
_____
_____
_____
_____

What brings me the most pleasure is:

_____
_____
_____
_____
_____
_____

Affirmation

"Even though

(fill in the blank with anything to do with your body or physical experience that you may be carrying negative feelings, thoughts, guilt, or shame about),

I am a sensual being and give myself permission to experience a pleasure."

Bonus Exercise!

Look at your body in a mirror. Tell your body, "I love you. Thank you for all you do for me. I promise to take good care of you." Send some extra love and affirmations to the areas of your body around which you experience judgment or wounds. For example: "I love you, thighs. You are big and strong and carry me through my life." If you want to get really adventurous, you can do this exercise naked.

Guided Meditation

Sit or lie down and make yourself comfortable. Take three long, deep, letting-go breaths, in through your nose and out through your mouth. Continue breathing in your own natural way. Begin to visualize yourself gazing upon your body as if you have an unconditional, nonjudgmental love of yourself. Imagine that you are sending love to your entire body. Feel your body begin to relax with this loving attention. Choosing to either simply bring your awareness to each body part or if you'd like, allow a loving touch to also be included as you move your awareness from body part to body part. Begin with your head and face, allowing a smile to come to your face. Move this gentle loving awareness from your face down to your neck and throat. Feel the sensation of your loving caress of attention down your arms and hands, then your chest, abdomen, pelvis, and hips, down your legs and feet. Feel the nurturing warmth of your own awareness radiating into the warmth of your skin. Send yourself love through every intention. When you are complete, notice how your body feels.

When you view your body as a beautiful temple that houses your soul, you will find it is your gateway to pleasure and joy.

Be One

*"You are not separate from the whole.
You are one with the sun, the earth, the air.
You don't have a life. You are life."*

~ Eckhart Tolle

Spiritual misfits often are intellectually aware of the concept of unity, that we are all one. However, they may not truly feel the connection. They may more often feel separate. They long for a connection to Spirit, and for their spiritual home, where they believe they came from. Their desire is understandable, yet unnecessary, as this connection is always available to them. Their feeling of separateness is only an illusion. They don't have to long for it anymore. It is right there, within them.

What are some symptoms of a person who is spiritually disconnected?

1. They spend significant time thinking about the problems in their lives.

2. They search for answers and meaning outside of themselves.

3. They are stuck in a place of waiting for the universe to give them a sign of what they are supposed to do with their lives.

4. They ignore their intuition.

5. They feel lonely.

6. They feel disconnected from their purpose.

7. They may be depressed or anxious.

8. They may rely on others for their spiritual connection, such as going to psychics or others whom they view to be more spiritually connected.

Let's look at an example:

Amanda was raised in a religious household and community. As a child, she felt close to God, the saints, and the angels. She felt God's presence through the rituals that the Catholic Church provided. During college, Amanda immersed herself in religious studies. While learning about other cultures and religions, she realized she no longer could believe all she had been taught within her Catholic upbringing. She stepped away from the church, its belief systems and ultimately her community. Although she felt comfortable in her decision, she also experienced a disconnection that left her questioning her identity and beliefs. She began feeling lonely, sad, and confused. She knew she needed to find faith again.

Amanda went on a journey of discovery to explore the world's religions and spirituality. She traveled to immerse herself in practices from various traditions as she sought truth and meaning. Gradually, she felt more and more drawn to the path of Christian mysticism. She discovered that the mystic's path weaves its way through the commonalities of all of the religious teachings. It became the bridge for her to reunite with her spiritual upbringing from this new-found spiritual maturity. She opened her heart back to Catholicism and reconnected to some of the spiritual rituals she had known and loved during her childhood. She began to feel her connection to God, the saints, and the angels again, this time with a fresh perspective. She writes about her experiences and aspires to share this wisdom with other people interested in the mystical path.

What will you experience when you are connected to all that is?

1. You feel connected to higher wisdom and allow your life to be governed by this wisdom.

2. You treat everyone with love and compassion.

3. You often can see the bigger picture of a situation.

4. Your life has meaning.

5. You exude peace.

6. You trust yourself to make decisions.

7. You trust others.

8. You have communion with Spirit.

A yogic master once said, "The greatest distance in the world is between the head and the heart." How does one not only mentally understand they are part of the fabric of the universe, yet also feel it, and know it is the very essence of their beings? The heart center (not the physical heart) but the home of heart energy, is the place within the human being that can transcend all time and space. It is the place that connects us to all that is. The path to feeling your connection with the Divine is to open your heart and allow the love that you have to merge with the love of the universe. How does one cultivate this?

The answer is through daily spiritual practice, whatever that looks like for you. This could be anything you do that helps you feel a union with the Divine. Some examples are breathwork, prayer, meditation, yoga, ritual, being in nature, creating art, dancing, or listening to music. The key is to find a way to do something that brings you joy and places you in a flow state. This flow state puts your mind at ease and ends distractions and worries. Here, the mind has space and stillness between thoughts, if there are any at all. It is in this space, in this stillness of the mind and with an open heart, that one can experience a connection to the Divine.

Journaling Exercise

Complete the following sentences:

How I feel most connected is:
_____
_____
_____
_____
_____
_____

The thing that brings me the most peace is:
_____
_____
_____
_____
_____
_____

The best place for me to find a sense of community is:
_____
_____
_____
_____
_____
_____

Get Connected!

Some spaces for spiritual misfits to find their tribe are: non-secular and progressive churches, such as Unitarian Universalist, Unity churches, or Quaker friends meetings. Meditation circles, Yoga communities, Zen centers, and New Age stores that offer classes. Shamanic or pagan circles, mind/body/spirit festivals and spiritual retreats are also possible sources of community for misfits.

Affirmation

"Even though I may not always feel the Divine (or replace with your word, God, Spirit, etc.),

I know the Divine is within me

and there for me always."

Guided Meditation

Find a comfortable position and close your eyes. Take three long, deep breaths, in through your nose and out through your mouth. Adjust your body until you are completely relaxed and comfortable. Allow your breathing to become calm and steady. Begin to visualize a beautiful glowing gold light above the crown of your head.

This light represents calmness, peace, and higher wisdom. As you inhale, visualize this golden light coming in through the crown of your head and making its way all the way down your body. As you exhale, send this light out through your feet. With each inhale, you draw more golden light from above, bathing your entire body. With each exhale, you send it out through your feet. Continue.

Now, allow yourself to rest your awareness at the soles of your feet. Imagine here luminous silver light. This light represents nurturing and supportive Mother Earth energy. As you inhale, draw this vibrant silver light up through the soles of your feet, and all the way up through your entire body. As you exhale, send this energy out through the crown of your head. Bathe your entire energy field with it and let it flow back down to the Earth. With each inhale you draw more supportive, grounding energy from the Earth all the way up your body.

With each exhale, send this energy out through the crown of your head, bathing your body and your energy field all the way back down to the Earth. Now imagine with every breath that you are simultaneously drawing energy from both places, above and below. These energies begin to merge and dance at your heart. Imagine now that this energy forms a perfect white light.

Now with each exhale, you imagine that light growing bigger, expanding into every cell of your body. Expanding even more quickly now, you imagine that light growing and expanding into your energy field, including all the space that surrounds you.

Soon, the white light expands beyond your energy field. It begins to travel, connecting you with the world. With every breath, the light continues to expand beyond our world into our solar system, beyond our solar system into the center of the universe. Allow yourself to feel at unity with the universe.

When you are ready, keeping this feeling of oneness with you, begin to make your way back through our solar system and to our world. To your body rest-

ing and begin to breathe deeply again. Wriggle your fingers and toes and stretch in any way that feels comfortable to you. When you are ready, open your eyes.

When we allow ourselves to recognize that we are one with all that is, we release judgment. We allow ourselves to live in a state of open-hearted compassion and unity.

Align Yourself with Your Purpose

"Your life has a purpose. Your story is important.
Your dreams count. Your voice matters.
You were born to make an impact."

~ Author Unknown

Spiritual misfits usually know they are here on Earth for a reason, even if they do not know what that reason is. Some people seem to be born knowing exactly what they are here to do. Most of us are not so lucky. We must find our purposes through trial and error, through life experiences. Living life on purpose and having a mission, something we feel passionate about is an integral part of having happiness here on Earth. What do our lives mean? Why are we here? What are we supposed to be doing with our time here? How can we best contribute to making the world a better place? These are all good questions to ask ourselves when we are trying to discover our purpose.

Spiritual misfits often have the idea, belief, or hope that the universe or Spirit will tell them what their purpose is. They feel that if they wait, they will be given signs that will lead them along the right path. Can this happen? Sure, it can. There are many stories of people who were given signs, followed them, and were led to a beautiful path of happiness and fulfillment. Does this happen for everyone? No. Should we wait on the universe to tell us what to do? We could, but this leaves us in a place of disempowerment.

Some spiritual misfits get stuck for years in this unhappy place of uncertainty, waiting for something outside of themselves to tell them what to do. What if the universe wants us to figure it out? Often, the journey we take is a path of our own choosing. We must leap into a self-made choice, not knowing if it is the right decision and embark upon a road with an unknown outcome. Sometimes we must risk the possibility of making a "wrong" choice to give us forward momentum, and to be a step closer to finding our purpose.

Let's look at an example:

Susan is a compassionate and heart-centered person. She grew up in a small suburban community and inherently had an interest in people who were different from her. She felt empathy and compassion for the few ethnically diverse students at her school, who were often the victims of bullying. She continued to witness, and later was herself a target of this harassment when, as an adult, she married someone of different ethnic background and had multiracial children. Believing strongly in the values of equality and justice, she feels angry when she is confronted with any act or comment she views to be unfair or prejudiced to any group of people.

Susan is in a stage of life where she has some freedom to explore herself and embark upon a second career. Her children are grown and she has retired from her previous career. She does not have to work and struggles to know what to do with herself or her time. She dreams of starting a non-profit organization that helps educate people and eradicates racism, yet doesn't know if that is what she is "meant to do" or "supposed to do." She often goes to psychics with one burning question, "What is my purpose?" She gets some ideas for writing a book through these mediums, yet knows that's not the answer she is looking for. She wants certainty about what she is supposed to be doing, and when she doesn't have it, she feels immobilized. She is waiting for a sign from God because she does not want to make the wrong choice for her life. Susan carries on this way for years, feeling frustrated and unfulfilled.

She eventually gets tired of waiting and being frustrated. She knows she needs to face her fear of making the wrong choice. She chooses to spend some time working on an issue she is passionate about as a way to do something worthwhile and meaningful with her time.

She steps out by organizing a social justice committee at her church. She gathers together like-minded people who also have a passion for equality. They begin to make an impact in their community through volunteering educational opportunities with children.

Susan, much to her surprise, also decides to write a children's book about equality and justice. Susan still dreams of starting a non-profit, yet is happy and fulfilled with her community volunteer efforts and with her creative book endeavor. Susan is now living her life on purpose. She no longer seeks out guidance from psychics or frets over what to do with her life. She is too busy living it.

With Susan, we can clearly see she was stuck in indecision. She was waiting for validation to come from outside of herself to tell her what to do. She was disempowered, not living her life or making her own choices. By choosing not to choose, she was choosing nothing. Susan was allowing her fear to control her. This is never what the Divine intends for us. We must experience life to its fullest, be willing to risk, be willing to fail, be willing to live! As in Susan's case, her answers were right in front of her all along. She just did not see them until she was ready.

Often, the way to our purposes is through our strife and our struggles. Our biggest life challenges often have our purposes woven into them. If we can make it through to the other side of the struggle, we then have a gift to share. We have the understanding, the compassion, the knowing of how to help others along the same path. We carry medicine that can heal, can teach, can mentor, can guide, can serve.

How do we know what our purposes are? One of the clues is to look at your life experiences. Is there an experience or pattern that was difficult for you? Did you make it through? Do you feel a passion to help others with similar struggles or to prevent the struggles in the first place? Another clue is to remember who we were as children. Sometimes as children, we are more connected to what we want to do with our lives than when we are adults.

Let's look at an example:

Ryley was an introverted child who struggled with social anxiety and depression. She was incredibly creative and could often be found in the comfort of her art, drawing. As she continued through her childhood, she grew in her identity of being an artist and developed a love for women's fashion as well. During her college years, she attempted to pursue an art therapy degree, but the stress of college along with her social anxiety and depression led her to drop out.

She traveled for a while in her 20's and worked meaningless temporary jobs. In her early 30's, she recalled a memory that was at the root of her anxiety and depression. This recall led her to begin counseling, in which she learned coping skills and experienced healing.

Although it was not easy for her, as she still struggled with social anxiety, she went back to school and graduated with her art therapy degree. She now works part-time as an art therapist and teaches art classes on the side. She also happily works a few hours a week at a boutique women's clothing store, helping women assemble fabulous outfits that help them feel good about themselves. Ryley finally feels at home, like she is living out the life she is supposed to live.

Another pitfall that spiritual misfits can encounter when trying to find their purpose is that they want to connect their purpose with their jobs or careers. These can be connected, as in Ryley's example, but they don't have to be. Perhaps a person has a job that is neutral to them, yet provides them with stability and takes care of their financial needs. Their purpose, though, lies in their volunteer work, such as fostering animals from a rescue. Just because someone does not get paid for their purpose does not mean that is not their purpose. If you have a passion but can't figure out how to make money at it, do it anyway. Make money a different way. You'll still be living your passion and living a life of purpose.

Another misconception that people have is that their purpose is just one thing. This idea of only having one purpose is a limiting belief. The truth is that our purposes change over time. For example, a child's purpose is often to grow and to get an education. As we become adults, this purpose changes. As we have families, our purpose changes again, and so forth. We can have many purposes in our lives. Living by this truth is important as it will allow you to see what your purpose is in your life right now, rather than longing for something that might be in the future. When we do this, we risk missing the opportunity that is right here, right now. So, even if you do not yet know your calling or know what direction you want to go in life, you can live a life of intention and purpose.

Let your purpose be to become the best version of yourself, spreading goodness, love, and kindness everywhere you go. Let every step you take and every interaction you have to be a purposeful reflection of the highest and best version of yourself. After all, isn't the awakening of the authentic self truly worthy of our attention and purpose? Allow your purpose to become more about who you are versus what you do. The answers about what you are to do will more easily and organically come to you when you are living out of this place of alignment and authenticity.

Journaling Exercise

Complete the following sentences.

What I feel most passionate about is:
_____
_____
_____

If passion feels difficult to you, try this:
What I am interested in is:
_____
_____
_____

The challenges I have overcome in my life are:
_____
_____
_____

I feel most joyful when I am:
_____
_____
_____

My best qualities are:
_____
_____
_____

Affirmation

Take a look at the statements on the previous page and use your answers to complete a personal mission statement to assist you in becoming the person you desire to be in the world.

"I am a _____

using my gifts of _____

to_____."

Examples:

"I am a courageous, grounded, and heart-centered person using my gifts of intuition and life experiences to help people heal and grow."

"I am a brave, bold and compassionate woman, wife and mother, who uses her strength, love, and wisdom to nurture her children, her husband and herself to become the best version of themselves."

Even if you don't believe your statement to be true yet, I encourage you to use it! Reciting it to yourself several times a day, like a mantra, will assist you in manifesting it into being.

Guided Meditation

Find a comfortable position, either lying down or sitting. Close your eyes and take a few deep, letting-go breaths. Begin to visualize yourself five years from now. Imagine that you are living a life in which you are happy and at peace, experiencing your best self. Observe what you look like, feel like and are doing. Become aware of any steps that led you there. Allow the experience to be visceral. Take your time. When you are ready, feel free to open your eyes.

Insights from the meditation:

___

___

___

___

___

___

___

___

___

___

___

___

Bonus exercise!

Use your personal mission statement and notes from the meditation to create a vision board. You'll need a poster board, magazines, glue stick, and scissors. Put your personal mission statement in the center of the board along with a symbolic representation of you. Cut out images and words that reflect the life you would like to create for yourself. Display your vision board to remind yourself of who you really are and the life you are creating for yourself.

"Never forget how wildly capable you are.
Believe in yourself.
You are a Star!"

~Author unknown

AFTERWORD

The Author's Journey

As a child, I remember having a deeply personal relationship with God, Jesus, and the angels and I felt most connected and at peace when I was alone spending time in nature. In retrospect, I was a spiritual misfit. I spent the majority of my early years feeling very different from others. When I was with a group of people, feelings of not belonging were ever-present. I believe a small part of this feeling of isolation was from being an introverted, empathic and intuitive child. However, the degree of social anxiety I experienced was the result of a disconnection in my body, mind, and soul, which had been caused by the shame of early childhood traumas.

Sad and confused, I longed to be understood and accepted, to feel loved and taken care of, and to simply feel okay with myself. This longing controlled me from my childhood into my young adult years. I wanted desperately to find what I was looking for outside of myself. Although I had maintained a relationship with God, I was on a path that was filled with fear, confusion, mistakes, heartaches, dysfunction, and pain.

The journey back to myself has not been an easy one but has been the best choice I could have ever made. Once I chose a path of healing, I faced the pain I had been avoiding and became conscious of how my wounds were controlling me. I learned how to let go of the past and to live present in my body and in the moment. I broke down the protective barriers that I had built up around myself; that were not only separating me from others but had grown to disconnect me from myself.

The commitment to wholeness has taken strength, courage, bravery, vulnerability, and humility.

This emergence has involved a multi-facted process of:

1. Facing my fears.

2. Being present in my body.

Afterword

3. Forgiving myself and others.

4. Accepting and having compassion with myself.

5. Learning how to love and be loved.

6. Using my voice.

7. Stepping into my power.

8. Letting go of my Ego's attempts to control and surrendering to the Divine.

After the burning away of the parts of myself that no longer served me, my true self emerged. And, like the phoenix rising out of the ashes, I was reborn with wings to fly.

Now, I no longer feel *not from here* as there is nowhere else I would rather be. I love the feeling of connectedness with myself, others and the earth. I find so much joy in being rooted in community, friendships, and family. This was the greatest gift I could have ever given myself. To be here now, in my body, spiritually connected, heart opened wide, feet firmly planted on the ground, and living my life on purpose. I have arrived and am present in my life.

Now, that certainly doesn't mean that life is perfect without challenges, as there are plenty of them. It also doesn't mean that I don't fall short. I am imperfectly human, after all. What it does mean is that I have the tools and the foundation to be brave and show up for myself and in my life; and my journey, like all of ours, is still ever-evolving. It has been and continues to be a divine orchestration of the right people, situations, and tools that have led me to where I am; all of which I am so very grateful for. In retrospect, I can see Spirit has been alive and active in my life; assisting me in moving toward a path of wholeness long before I was aware such a journey existed.

The modalities I have used to support my path were counseling, bodywork, creative movement, energy healing, yoga, tantra, meditation, breathwork, and shamanism. I spent six years immersed in a system of self-actualization techniques, Ipsalu Tantra Kriya Yoga, that consisted of retreats and recommended daily spiritual practices of movement, breathwork, and meditation techniques. This system was my most transformative and powerful healer. I went on to discover The Shamanic Priestess Process, which was a system of healing, empowerment, and self-discovery. It was within this system that I healed

Afterword

my disconnection to the Divine Feminine and came into my personal power, learning how to be a channel of my gifts to the world.

Writing and self-help books have played a significant role in my journey as well. Here is a shortlist of important authors and books that have been influential to me:

Animal Speak
 by Ted Andrews

A Return to Love
 by Marianne Williamson

Atlas of the Heart
 by Brene Brown

Autobiography of a Yogi
 by Paramahansa Yogananda

Autobiography of an Orgasm
 by Betsy Blankenbarger

Awaken the Giant Within
 by Tony Robbins

Be Here Now
 by Ram Dass

Big Magic
 by Elizabeth Gilbert

Burnout
    by Emily and Amelia Nagoski
Chakras and their Archetypes
    by Ambika Wauters
Codependent No More
    by Melanie Beatty
Conversations with God
    by Neale Donald Walsch
Emotional Agility
    by Susan David
Fearless Living
    by Rhonda Britten
Healing the Shame that Binds You
    by Gary Bradshaw
Intuitive Healing
    by Judith Orloff
Jewel in the Lotus
    by Sunyata Saraswati and Bodhi Avinasha
Keeping the Love You Find & Getting the Love You Want
    by Harville Hendrix
One Day My Soul Just Opened Up
    by Iyanla Vanzant

Afterword

Recovery of Your Inner Child
 by Dr. Lucia Capachionne

Sacred Contracts
 by Carolyn Myss

The Artist Way
 by Julia Cameron

The Body is Not an Apology
 by Sonja Renee Taylor

The Body Keeps the Score
 by Bessel van der Kolk

The Dance of the Dissident Daughter & The Mermaid Chair
 by Sue Monk Kidd

The Dark Side of the Light Chasers
 by Debbie Ford

The Five Languages of Love
 by Gary Chapman

The Four Agreements
 by Don Miguel Ruiz

The Gifts of Imperfection
 by Brene Brown

The Hero with a Thousand Faces
 by Joseph Cambell

The Ipsalu Formula; a Method for Tantra Bliss
   by Bodhi Avinasha

The New Earth
   by Ekhart Tolle

The Road Back to You
   by Ian Morgan Cron and Suzanne Stabile

The Seven Habits of Highly Effective People
   by Steven Covey

The Untethered Soul
   by Michael Singer

Untamed
   by Glennon Doyle

What Happened to You?
   by Oprah Winfrey and Bruce D. Perry

What Makes Love Last?
   by John Gottman

Women Who Run with the Wolves
   by Clarissa Pinkola Estes

Women's Wisdom Women's Bodies
   by Dr. Christiane Northup

You Can Heal Your Life
   by Louise Hay

Afterword

If you are interested in learning more information about the two transformative processes I mentioned in my journey visit www.ipsalutantra.org and www.goddessontheloose.com.

These were the tools of transformation that worked for me, so I included them in case they might work for you too. I encourage you to follow your heart and intuition to guide you to the resources and experiences that are ripe with opportunity for you. Even if you don't actively pursue personal growth, I believe every experience you have in life can be a teacher, if you are a student who pays attention and is open to the lesson.

Remember you have the power to choose who you want to be in any given moment and there are many ways to experience the best version of yourself. You have your unique path to walk and to discern what that is for you.

Whatever path you choose, may you walk connected to your inner light. May you love deeply. May you have peace within and a grateful, joyful heart. From my heart to yours, may you live a life you love!

Thank you for reading and allowing me to share of myself and my journey with you.

~ Laura Rain

Did you enjoy this book?

Do you feel you benefitted in some way by reading it?

Tell me about it by writing a review wherever you bought this book.

Knowledge — Pass it on!

Thanks for sharing!

Are you looking for a community?
You can connect with me and other
spiritual misfits by joining my community!

Be sure to visit me at

www.holisticspiritualcounseling.com

About the Author

Laura Rain is a holistic spiritual counselor who helps people heal using a mindfulness-based, somatic approach. She has been in practice since 2005 and works with individuals, couples, and groups.

Laura contributes to the health and wellness field through writing and speaking engagements related to holistic healing and mindfulness.

Laura loves spending time with her family and friends, communing with nature, traveling, writing, and living a healthy active lifestyle.

To connect with Laura, visit her at:
www.holisticspiritualcounseling.com

www.ingramcontent.com/pod-product-compliance
Lightning Source LLC
Chambersburg PA
CBHW070105080526
44586CB00013B/1193